Because I Care, a title in the Tiny Tea series

© 2001 by Dee Appel

Published by Blue Cottage Gifts™, a division of Multnomah Publishers, Inc.

P.O. Box 1720, Sisters, OR 97759

ISBN 1-58860-028-9

Artwork by Gay Talbott Boassy

All works of art reproduced in this book are copyrighted by Gay Talbott Boassy and may not be reproduced without the artist's permission. For more information regarding art featured in this book, please contact:

> Mr. Gifford B. Bowne II
> Indigo Gate, Inc.
> 1 Pegasus Drive
> Colts Neck, NJ 07722
> (732) 577-9333

Designed by Koechel Peterson & Associates, Minneapolis, Minnesota

Scripture quotation taken from *The Holy Bible*, New International Version ©1973, 1984 by International Bible Society, used by permission of Zondervan Publishing House.

Printed in China

01 02 03 04 05 06 —10 9 8 7 6 5 4 3 2 1 0

www.bluecottagegifts.com

Because I Care

TEXT BY DEE APPEL   ART BY GAY TALBOTT BOASSY

BLUE COTTAGE GIFTS™
a division of Multnomah Publishers, Inc.
Sisters, Oregon

*B*ecause *I* care,
I'll always be

as close as any phone.

*B*ecause *I* care,
*T*here is no need
to ever feel alone.

The days to come may be hard,
I pray you won't despair.

Please know how
very much you're loved,
And that your burden's shared.

Don't believ

much what alw

hae

the

summer.

for me

he entire

w

your

ratur. their d

ie

but imagine

for

thought the u

ll

Draw strength from those

who love you—

I'm sure we'd all agree,

You need to take
some time for you,
And brew a cup of tea.

*If I could
I'd be right there
each moment of the day.*

To hold your hand

And give support,

To help in any way.

But even if I'm far away,
Or if I can't be there,

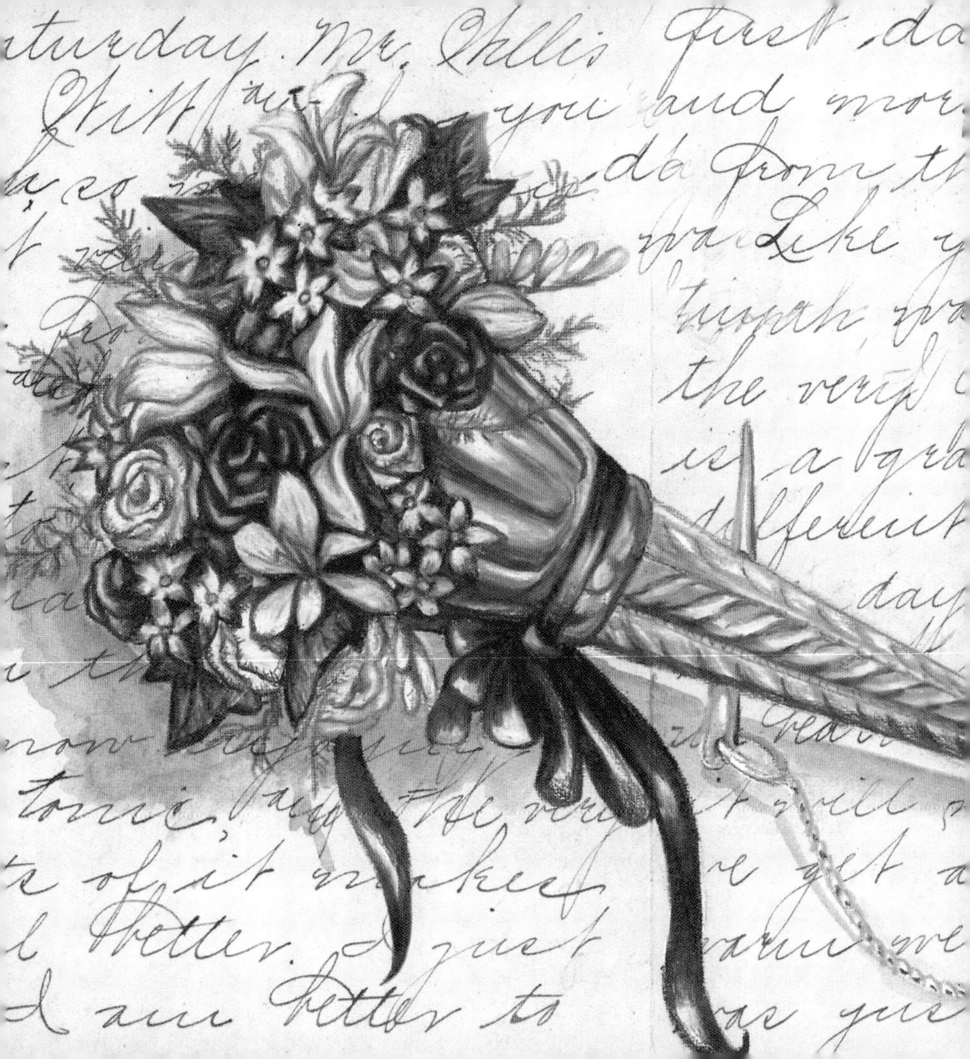

You know my heart
is always near,
Because I really care.

Carry each other's burdens.

❧

Galatians 6:2